On a remote forest farm in northern Sweden, the static of Lars Ruth's unsettled mind is fizzing. Voices. Sightings. Encounters, real and imagined, hint at a fractured and fragmentary life. Something is falling apart – something coming together.

The Invention of Lars Ruth is an intimate, visionary exploration of psychic disquiet. Its themes, of remembrance and aloneness, spiral around an evasive, haunting figure. But who is Lars? His voice is the echo to a volatile mind, aware of its disintegration, fearful of imminent collapse. Only by re-imagining his place in the natural world and the mysterious creatures in it, can Lars Ruth secure his newly awakening self.

Previous publications by George Messo

Poetry
Violades & Appledown, 2012
Hearing Still, 2009
Entrances, 2006
From the Pine Observatory, 2000

Translations
Orhan Veli: *Complete Poems*, 2016
İlhan Berk: *The Book of Things*, 2016
İlhan Berk: *New Selected Poems 1947–2008*, 2016
Contemporary Turkish Women Poets, 2015
İlhan Berk: *Letters & Sounds*, 2014
Birhan Keskin: *& Silk & Love & Flame*, 2013
Gonca Özmen: *The Sea Within*, 2011
İkinci Yeni: The Turkish Avant-Garde, 2009
İlhan Berk: *Madrigals*, 2008

George Messo

The Invention of Lars Ruth

Poems

Shearsman Books

First published in the United Kingdom in 2021 by
Shearsman Books Ltd
PO Box 4239
Swindon
SN3 9FN

Shearsman Books Ltd Registered Office
30–31 St. James Place, Mangotsfield, Bristol BS16 9JB
(this address not for correspondence)

www.shearsman.com

ISBN 978-1-84861-706-3

CONTENTS

The Invention of Lars Ruth

Cuckoo Taiga

"Who, travelling through the void,
does the breath-spent here,
to one among the worlds, translate?"

—Paul Celan,
translated by Ian Fairley

THE INVENTION OF LARS RUTH

Lars & Lars

When Lars Ruth
came to visit

he said
first
someone else is here

who
        you've never met
and second

he's in me
by which

                I mean
let's find

the other you
to greet him

and the four
of us sat

at this very table
Lars there and me

fingering my tie
exchanging glances

Oared

The foetus knows everything
said Lars
but slips from its dark
into ignorance
                              like a boat
drifting over a shoal.

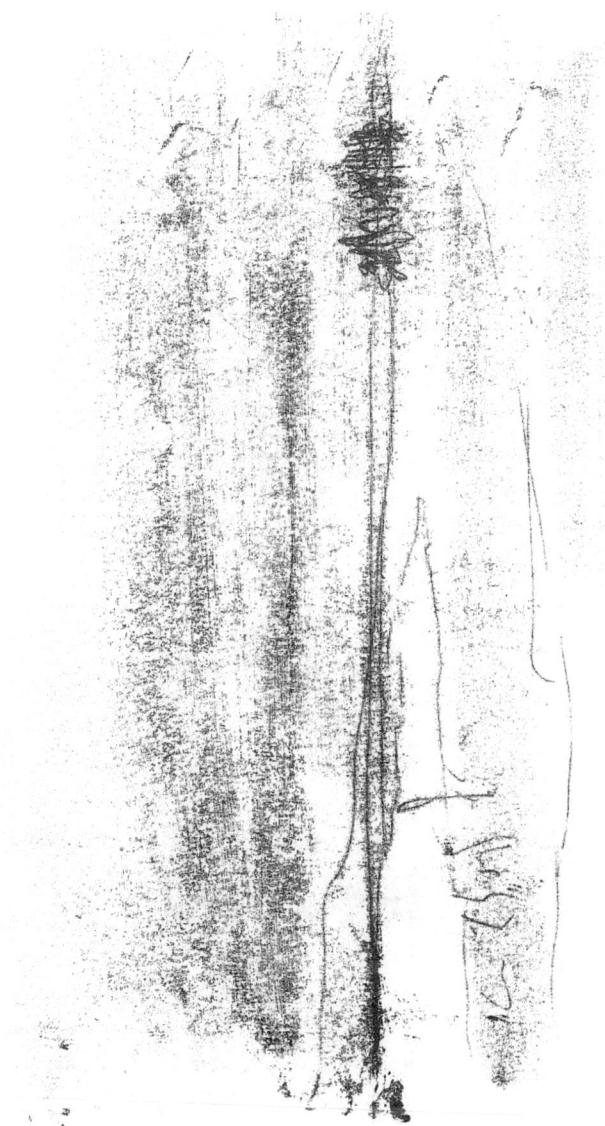

Lockers and Lars

The lake's ingenuity
for hiding things.

A Dwelling Place for Lars

We sat
with morning in the room

until the grey walls turned blue
and the breath went out of him.

No slowing down
or sudden exhalation

of a dying wish. Just
my father, dead.

And when I drew the blind
all the breathing creatures

were gathered
and pressed to the window.

Yes and No to Everything

Clouds across the lake
like a bad mood sealed
inside an envelope.

News arrived
down networks
of the inaudible.

Small filled space
becoming weather.

Incognito

In Ottoman poems
I have observed

the concluding stanza
typically carries

the poet's name,
a signature of sorts

and what is more
Lars Ruth,

whose reedy breath
plays like wind

through derelict rooms,
has often heard it said

*all language is a longing
for home*

Welcome

Coming home
sunlight's door into the dark
half closed half open

I see myself
clearly indistinct
against the background

of an overwhelming thought
going home,
going deeper.

Go

Looking for a lost friend
you follow a path

deep in the throat
of a silent forest.

Late and by yourself
you come to a wide river,

on the far bank
the empty boat is tethered.

Now that you know where he is
how are you going to reach him

Visioning Lars

At night
alone in the forest,
a vast breathing.

You stumble
on the sudden wealth
of a ruin.

A Lars of sights and smells

Those dry late winter mornings
when mud lies baked on roadsides

and on tyres and flicks off
leaving a broken trail where the tractor

shudders into life and moves away.
That's what I like.

Lars in his Library of Forgetting

Essentially
his scholarship of broken bowls
and vanishing signs

shows himself his labyrinth.
But still he's there
because

some lend, his friends,
their pliant weight
against his path:

them struggle and leave,
then reappear again.

Poems Lars

Going, there is a letter.
Clearly you can read between the lines.
An open door, its tone is mostly wonder.

Years ago we found you laughing here
and piling stones into a poem.

Autumn Lars

A thought grows deep inside the apricot.
A thousand miles from here
hoar frost dusting an arctic scythe.

CUCKOO TAIGA

Painting the Barn Doors

The wooden house
adjusts its memory.

A stubborn wind
would break these brittle stars

of frosted marram; the short-lived
seed heads stiff with age and ice

will fall
to where you left the frozen brushes

overnight. *I know*
there is a moon in you

but I cannot see it. The more
I press, the more the bristles part.

Clearings I

You follow a path
laid by many
but in the end
you are alone
where trees crowd
to a scene
of accidental loss.

On a Journey by Canoe

The tyranny of a lake's vast hypothesis
rose against me as the old boat

broke free of its jetty —
setting out, otter-blade drawn, thoughts

carried away, and you momentarily free
of the body.
>   *Lakeness from the lake.*

Treeness from the tree.
>   *Oneness from the one.*
The enigma, easily seen but unreachable.

Clearings II

Morning leaves the wing
feathers perfectly oiled
sinews at the collar
tattered, reeking faintly.

The mystery of his death
spirals high on thermals
over us, then suddenly pulls away.
One bird to kill another.

Crane

A pendulum
swings through the marsh,
bridging cracks in the dark.

If we adjust the light
you can understand his message
without knowing what you've learnt.

Siege of Lars

Exhalation
of dry leaves
crunched under
feet that fly.

*

A steady
thop
makes overnight
a bed of fallen apples.

*

We sleep in meadows.
Darkness breaks out and surrounds us.

One ear pressed to earth,
one to the cosmos.

Lumens, Late One Summer Afternoon

His once voice, fading birdlike, many facts upon him. Frequencies of air and light, captured by a moving leaf-spectacle of a flickering canopy.

I ask if you're there, only when I know you are, unlearning daily the loveliness of a world without me, life curved like a question mark, or a sickle, blinded momentarily, as if it meant something.

Lars Smoke

The books were cold. Pages foxed. Lime stains tracing mysterious clouds like Japanese picture books. The kind of clouds you could sit on. Decay of torn spines, rotting glue, whiff of graves and libraries; a spectacle, borderline baroque.

Now and then an opened book released a scent the room had long forgotten.

Often he sat with darkness crowding to the amber glow of his pipe, light from a streetlamp catching the rising smoke.

Possibilities and Solutions

The winter of zero two he lived in a concertina of discordant harmonies. He couldn't argue. The drugs said yes to everything. Springs, levers, fluted pipes. But calmly, quietly, yes to nevertheless, an elegant mix of compromise. In those days Lars was a laminated key passing himself off as ivory.

A House in the Forest

No one came. But words led and you followed. I could see it was raining inside the house. I knew Lars would be happy there, the incalculable slowness of its ruminant mind, for now a sanctuary, a place of gathering, of falling endlessly towards the august light.

We unlocked the door and stepped inside. "I'm so glad you came," he said.

A Poem by Solveig von Schoultz
translated by Lars Ruth

The lantern carried its light trembling through the forest;
rough hooves shifted beneath their weight; a beam

quivered over the white of an eye and passed on,
sealed the dark like the zip on a body bag.

Denning

Today we disappear.
Taste for tiny space.
Marsupial warmth.
My favourite place
to hide is here in you.

Cupboards. Undersides
of stairs and beds.
In fields where blankets
tossed on rusted frames
of prams are dens

for wintering out.
Boxes. Crates. We wear them all,
Unseen. Hiding still.
Today we disappear –
in dust clouds

blown from old quarries
- as if, on the other hand,
we'd simply walked away,
sky like old polythene
and you without a shadow.

Boats at Wick

What evidence there is for Turner's use of tempera – quail egg yolk, a drop of Gum Arabic – rests entirely with the bluebottle.

Beneath an ochre wash, the faint whiff of foetus.

Who didn't use temperas in those days? But quail? Cuckoo? Wren? These days Lars is all about bluebottles and the egg temperas used in Turner's watercolours. For instance, and this from the artist's notes: ignoring an overlooked cheese sweating in its porcelain dish, a bluebottle lands repeatedly on 'Boats at Wick'. Turner is puzzled. At first, so are we, not least because no such work can now be found among his many watercolour sketches.

Puzzlement, then, but a gradual widening of the iris. Could it be, further to its sense of smell and taste, the fly can actually *see*, as it were, from beneath the rapid strokes of Prussian Blue, the unborn cuckoo taking flight?

What does it matter that we ourselves can no longer see this luminous sketch or ascertain the precise chemistry of its composition?

Notes on Character

Aching. Breathless. Broken.
Modulations rise like summer heat.
Your beautiful schizophrenia.

In *me* I find unfathomable *you*:
down into the well,
the heart leaving its body.

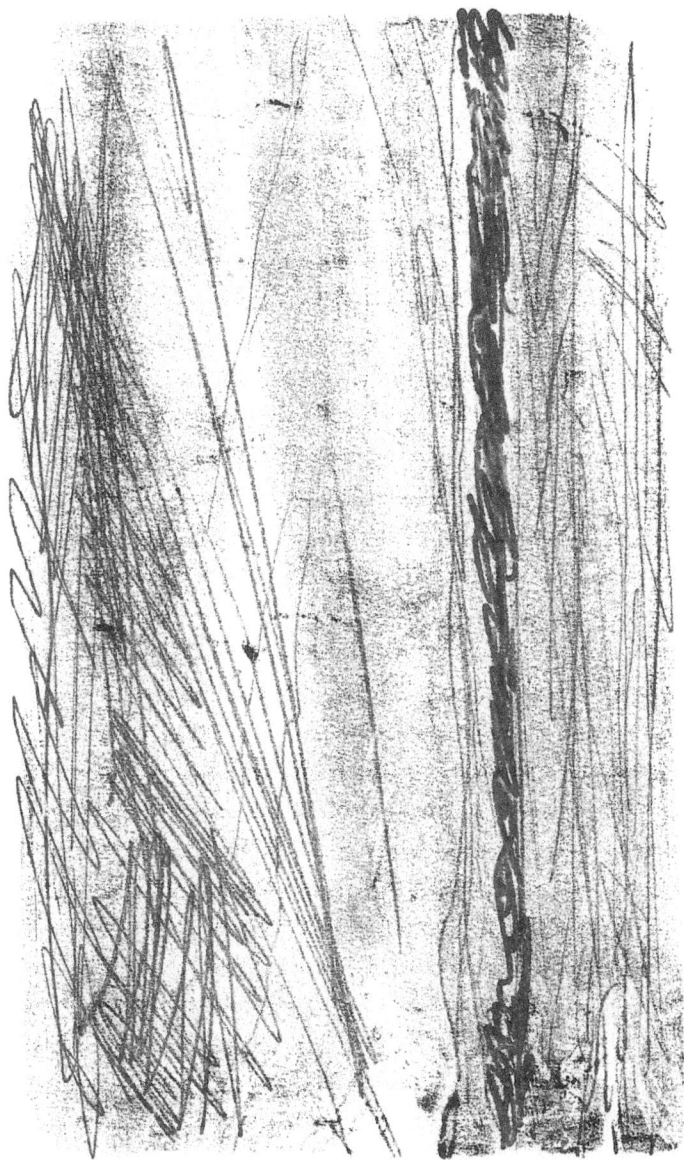

Horses in a Field

What are they doing
their unkeeled forms
like barges
inching through
a swollen current?

Always by the alders
but no one rides them.

Then there were no horses.
The alders had gone.
The field had gone.

The field had gone.

Three Eggs Lars

I stumbled into madness like a forest clearing;
ran down scales of a small irresolute fugue, my
shirts caught in the cog wheels of a vast wooden
clock. The analogies were endless. I could go
on but in the end it was inevitable I would find
myself in that micro cosmos where everything
spoke a foreign language.

So I was obsessed with the abstruse algebra of
crack formation, a tricky business but full of
openings. That's when I came down and saw
there were three eggs in a terracotta bowl.

No straight lines. No corners.
An exhausting kinaesthesia of detail.
There were eggs and there was a bowl.
Something marvellous would soon begin.

I walked to the table and opened a large notebook
marked "Poems: first drafts." On a scruffy page
black with hasty jottings and crossings-out the
words "Three Eggs" in which it seemed to say my
accident of circumstance was not a consequence
foretold. Illness. A loosening of the bolts. A
lesion slowly forcing the fabric apart but not
unlike a curtain also drawn to show three eggs
in a terracotta bowl and what they said spoke
somehow more than the words used to say it,
whatever that was.

Cuckoo Taiga

Air, falling at dusk
in small summer hours
pushes through boreal
spruce its huge voice.

Recovery

Vårt sorgespel är slut.

—*Harry Martinson*

Early morning teaches touch.
Go over again the wet grass
fingers gently numb and
tap on rain in tiny globes
about a Lady's Mantle.

The self is never the same.
By increments senses shape
themselves around a leaf.
You're not a name but naming
sounds a same wind

breathing you and the rest
folds inward like a star,
implosion's serried light
accents a deeper dark.

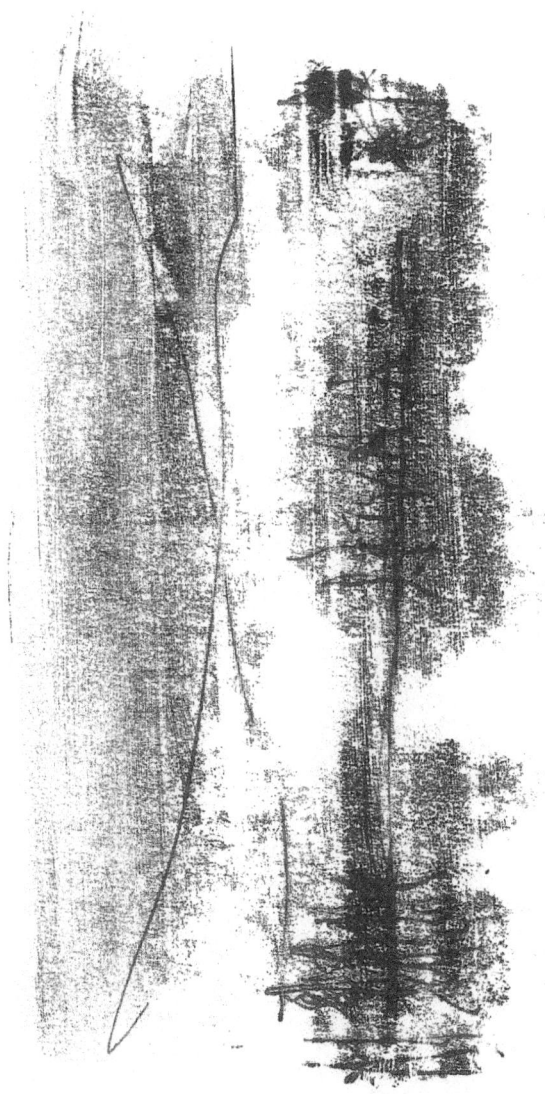

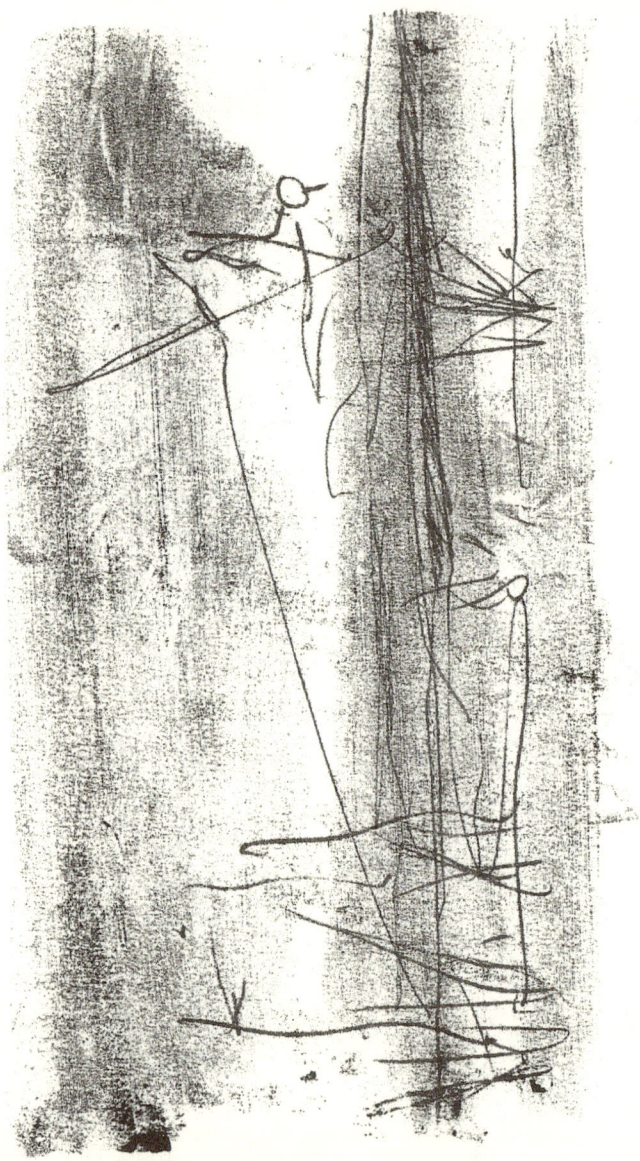

Fog's Room-size Acoustics

For years I ran around. Oiled cleaned greased
wound. Sweated over pendulums, cogs, springs.
Then one day all the alarm clocks in the house
went off at once. Doctor Asger was sitting in the
living room. It was time to go. Something about
the grass told me it was over. Hints of ochre in the
changing light. The summer meadow, windswept,
wave-shifted, yellowing. I was ready to answer its
singular grammar, to rise, circle house and farm,
trailing filaments of air through fog's room-size
acoustics. Every preparation was made. At this
late hour I would never look back, and if I did it
was too dark to see the house disappear or busy
hands dismantling the forest.

Madness is like an incomparable simile but once
you've found your other, call him Lars.

Two Landscapes

I
Harvest,
as it once swept through the mead halls
of northern Europe, *hærfest, harbitas,*
hervist, herfst, haust, is a word
we seldom hear. In capitals
and municipal towns only the Old Norse,
harfr, meaning *to harrow.* Bodies
farmed for organs.

II
Autumn,
in the old High German *herbist,*
a time of gathering.

October fields. Birchwood's
scattered corpses.

The Art of Disappearing

You would not think to wake,
find deer grazing a meadow
metres away their unconcern and you
without regard for anything else.

Now would be a good time to start.
Watch closely, wait. Move
when they move, when eyelids
cut from memory – so you

perfectly there, cannot be seen –
a rock, a tree, indiscernible shade.
Pain is a voice without words –
hear it through a hole of silence.

Come Holy Spirit: all Song and no Story

Cloud-shift.
Fingers of light
sift through forests.

What's coming
will find its way.

It calls
and you recognise prints
across a cold field

but ignore them.
Your turning away
negates nothing.

The frozen cube
is a house
of gloomy embellishments,

rimless truth,
like an old church
deep inside a thicket,

tangled up in
distant cries and
plainsong.

Veni Sancte Spiritus.
Shadow has
its vespers too.

Whatevertheless

Somewhere:
Light-lines,
a filter to it;
leaf moulds,
needles
falling;

in destitute
ruts
the blood-rust
of autumn,
finches
high in their tree,
singing.

When
allissaidanddone,
our stories prevail –
songbirds dance
among ruins
and drag us
into the future.

Spectrograms

Silence is a myth except my house.
If I were still, repress the need
to talk although alone for weeks
and miles. I hear the scrape
of sleeves, pencil scratching
words across a page or

                              spectrograms in cold air
                              tracing breath, a pulse.
                              I take possession
                              of an orchestrated loss,
                              a wave you feel
                              but never hear. Silence.

The sudden thump a bird
on glass, dead
when I arrive, is now
a brambling, sweet lord,
the why of everything,
cooling in my hand.

Shoures Soote

Make for me
the few small nouns
breaking through
your April light

        a rainday
        holophrase.

Dogs – thank god they own someone –
are vomiting frozen air.
Their voices thaw and say:

We too are here. Wiser, faster.
Cloud makes everything audible
(and the will to lend yourself

its private ear): a drop of April rain.

Give us this day

'Þai grove a pitte byfore my face,
and þai felle þareinne.'
    —English Psalter, Psalm 56

I

Misdone to, then.
But bread's
uncrumbed wordiness
whole and hot tasting
sits on a table
boarded for four.

II

We, across the field,
smell faintly of shit
and perspiration,
meet with its drift.

III

The day is ours
but is no ones.
Are we right to sense
in dumb folds
your disengaging thoughts
forgetting us?

IV

Blue summer heat
lifts the earth.

We dig our pit
and throw ourselves

into it.

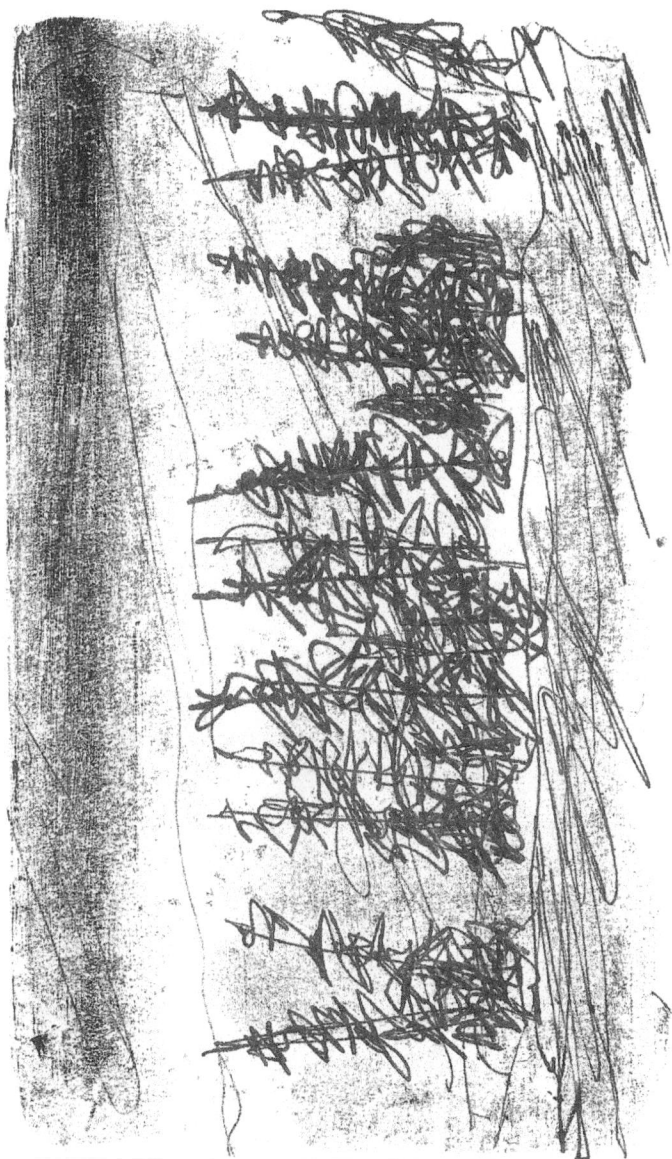

One Two Three

Fluoxetine. Bupropion. Lamotrigine.

I

Distant
and with light

wind
kneading dust

Trees
are skeletal

or bodies
tree-like

shuffling
or at rest

II

Sun   dis
integrates   me

the I
that sings

its trance-
like state

o wind
o wind

III

All
there is

of Lars

becoming

                              Lars

Lines at Palkovare

Getting there is easy
almost without trying
there is a river
audible brute particular
too large to be known

But in the afternoon
a powerful wind takes hold
birds are wrung from its pockets
darkness like wet leather
spreads over the earth

It is a knowing that isn't learnt
an invisible thread
leading you back through the maze
somewhere
you too will have your grave.

Acknowledgements

The author wishes to thank the editors of the following magazines, journals, and online sites where these poems originally appeared, sometimes in slightly different form:

Crossways: 'Horses in a Field'; *Eunoia Review*: 'Come Holy Spirit'; 'A Poem by Solveig von Schoultz'; *A Festschrift for Tony Frazer*: 'Lines at Palkovare'; *Molly Bloom*: 'Painting the Barn Doors,' 'Clearings I,' 'Clearings II,' 'Crane,' 'Siege of Lars'; *Poetry Salzburg Review*: 'Lars Smoke,' 'Possibilities and Solutions'; *Shearsman* magazine: 'Lars & Lars,' 'Oared,' 'Lockers and Lars,' 'A Dwelling Place for Lars,' 'Yes and No to Everything,' 'Incognito,' 'Welcome,' 'Go,' 'Visioning Lars,' 'A Lars of sights and smells,' 'Lars in his Library of Forgetting,' 'Poems Lars,' 'Autumn Lars'; *Snow lit rev*: 'Boats at Wick,' 'Three Eggs Lars,' 'Fog's Room-size Acoustics,' 'Spectrograms'; *Riggwelter*: 'Two Landscapes'

The following poems were also distributed through Daniel Kresh's monthly email poetry list: 'On a Journey by Canoe,' 'Lumens, Late One Summer Afternoon,' 'Denning,' 'Notes on Character,' 'Horses in a Field,' 'Recovery,' 'The Art of Disappearing,' 'Whatevertheless,' 'Shoures Soote,' and 'Give us this Day.'

Author Biography

George Messo is the author of three
previous collections of poems from
Shearsman Books, as well as volumes
of translated poetry. He was twice shortlisted for the European
Poetry Translation Prize and received a Hawthornden Fellowship
in 2001.

Messo studied Philosophy at London School of Economics,
Hull and Edinburgh, and holds a doctorate in Literary Translation
from UEA. He later studied drawing under Ilsa Brittain at the
University for the Creative Arts.

Born in Lincolnshire in 1969, Messo has lived and worked
for more than two decades in the Middle East. A former habitat
surveyor, mountaineer, cyclist, and fly-fishing and survival guide,
he now spends much of the year in northern Sweden where he
lives on a remote farm with his wife and children.

Messo's watercolours, oils and mixed media paintings can be
found at various locations online.

(Drawing of George Messo by Lawrence Ferlinghetti, 1992.)